SO YOU'RE LOOKING FOR A BUILDER

Peter Mikus

with a contribution by Dr Nada Trtnik

> How to Find the
> **Best Builder**
> for Your Job

TOTO PROPERTIES

ESCARPMENT PUBLISHING

So You're Looking for a Builder
Peter Mikus and Dr Nada Trtnik
Copyright © 2022
Published by Escarpment Publishing, Australia
ABN: 32736122056
https://escarpmentpublishing.com.au/

All rights reserved. No part of this publication may be reproduced, stored in a retrieval system or transmitted in any form or by any means electronic, mechanical, audio, visual or otherwise, without prior permission of the copyright owner. Nor can it be circulated in any form of binding or cover other than that in which it is published and without similar conditions including this condition being imposed on the subsequent purchaser.

ISBN: 978-1-922329-40-0
Book Design by K. Rose Kreative
Inside Cover Illustration by Ivy Mikus, with assistance from Juice Art Studio

Majority images used from Toto Properties.
Additional Images licenced for commercial use from Pixabay:
Concrete Image by Paul Harrison
Solar Panels by Ulrike Leone from Pixabay

Contents

Introduction	2
1 Who Can Be a Builder?	4
2 Where to Find a Builder	6
3 Should I Contact the Builder First or the Architect/Draftsman?	10
4 Can I Use a Square Metre Price to Estimate the Cost of My Project?	13
5 Should I Pay for a Quote?	15
6 How to Finance a Building Project	17
7 The Role of the Building Surveyor	20
8 The Difference Between Planning Permits & Building Permits	24
9 Disputes	26
10 Should I Engage an Independent Building Inspector?	28
11 Types of Building Projects	31
Decking	32
Excavations	34
Concreting	36
Brickwork	42
Landscaping	45
Pergolas	46
Bathroom or laundry renovation	48
Structural modifications	51
Extensions	54
Volume builders	56
Custom homes	58
Multi units	64
12 Energy Efficiency	67
Hydronic heating	72
Moisture management	74
Heating and cooling	78
The Insulation Go-to for Energy Saving	81
13 The Psychology Underlying our Decisions	84
About the Authors	97

"We are totally thrilled with our extension completed by Toto Properties. Peter and his trade teams delivered a quality build within the timeframe set. We particularly appreciated Peter's responsiveness to texts, emails and calls at all hours of the day and night. He was willing to accommodate our ideas and gave us good advice throughout the process. We are pleased with the quality of the finishes, including features like double glazing and square set plastering that were included as standard. Toto Properties guided us through the design process with their architect, Andrew, the permit requirements and the build itself. We have no hesitation in recommending them for your building projects."

– Joanne Cogan on Google reviews in January 2022.

Introduction

This review reflects the satisfaction every homeowner should aim for on completion of their building project. It is most likely the biggest financial investment one will make in their lifetime and, apart from that commitment, it also takes a substantial emotional toll. When looking for a builder, you will most likely search online and check reviews to see what other people have to say about a particular builder. If you pay attention, you will notice that no mention is made of money or price in reviews of the top-ranked builders. I learned early on in my career that whenever we tried to get a job by lowering the price, we rarely got a good review or a happy client. If you drop the price, you inevitably must cut corners to break even, and in the end nobody is happy. Does this mean that a good builder needs to be expensive? Not necessarily; I'm talking about a fair market price which will deliver a good product for the client and allow the builder modest profitability with a smooth supply chain and loyal subcontractors. This book is about how to get the most out of your builder and make the process as stress free as possible.

I'm Peter Mikus, director of Toto Properties Pty Ltd, a construction company specialising in projects on sloping sites and heavy-duty structural modifications. I've been involved in the building industry since my early childhood and a registered domestic builder in Victoria for the last ten years. We operate in Melbourne's eastern suburbs, and my legal knowledge is limited to Victorian law and low-rise residential building. Other jurisdictions have different laws and regulations, and every reader should consult with their local building authority.

During my building career, I have encountered many clients and had countless discussions about the building process. Clients seem to be more knowledgeable these days, mainly due to all the online resources available, but there are still many areas where critical and costly mistakes are made very early on, even before the design phase of a construction begins.

I wrote this book with the intention of helping people minimise potential financial loss and to save them time.

The design and construction process can also be very stressful, but we can minimise stress, eliminate it or even make the whole building project quite enjoyable. Tolerance for stress varies dramatically from one person to another. However, being well informed of what lies on the road ahead does help.

1
Who Can Be a Builder?

The short answer is ... everyone. However, we can clearly distinguish between two groups: registered builders and unregistered builders.

Are unregistered builders illegal? No. However, there are several limitations within which they can operate. All owner builders are in this category. Owner builders can build their own home (not an investment property) and they can build one project every three years. The other major category in this group is handymen or women doing small home improvements and maintenance. Generally, a building permit isn't needed for most small works below $10,000. However, there are a few exemptions; for example, house restumping does need a building permit, even below $10,000. Also, decking attached to the house needs a building permit regardless of the value of the project—decks are considered living areas and so are deemed to be house extensions. You should check with your local council or private building surveyor as to whether a building permit is needed for your proposed project.

Registered builders are divided into two main categories: domestic and commercial. This book is focused on domestic builders, which are further divided into subcategories of unlimited (DB-U) and limited (DB-L). The limitations can be to landscaping, verandas, bathrooms and so on.

The law in Victoria is currently changing, and soon carpenters will also need to be registered in line with other Australian states.

There is also a big grey area of 'builders' who sometimes do substantial works without being registered and sometimes without a building permit. They will try to convince homeowners to operate as owner builders and engage them as subcontractors. Be aware that with such an arrangement, all legal responsibility falls on your shoulders. If someone gets injured or killed on site, or if the building is not built as required by Australian building standards, future owners may sue you many years after you sell the property. For these reasons, you should avoid any such arrangement.

Your first question should be: Are you a registered builder?

2
Where to Find a Builder

These days the most obvious answer is the internet. However, I still get a considerable proportion of my jobs from people whose friends have recommended me, or people who live near my construction site and check on the work in progress, and a few of them just call me when driving behind one of our company vehicles. Some (mainly large) builders advertise on radio, TV or local cinema. Smaller builders also advertise in local newspapers. All the above options should be considered.

We will focus on the internet. Regardless of where you get your initial information, you should check out what you can find online. Specifically, check if the builder:
- Operates in your area
- Has good online feedback
- Has a presence on social media
- Does the type of job you're planning

You should aim to find a minimum of three builders to call, but preferably five or more.

There are several ways you can go about finding a builder, and you can use all of them. The most obvious is an internet search. You should type: 'builder' or 'building company', your suburb and the type of work you're looking for, such as 'renovation' or 'new house' or 'extension' or 'decking' or whatever best describes your proposed project. At the top of your search results will be builders with paid advertisements, followed by builders who are the best match for your search. Most builders who appear on the first page use some form of SEO (search engine optimisation) that helps get their listing on the first page. SEO services are provided by specialised companies who don't necessarily understand the construction industry, so I suggest checking the second and third page; real gems are usually hidden.

Between the builders on the first page of your search results, you'll also find free services such as Hi-pages and Oneflare. These services will provide you with three builders willing to quote on your job. These services are free for you (builders pay for it) and are a reasonably good source of quality builders. A good and reliable source is the Master Builders service, which provides a free list of builders operating in your area.

Case study

Years ago, on beginning my building career in Australia, I was looking at expanding my company, and I came across a client wanting a five-unit building. I desperately wanted to get this job to make some money and build up my reputation. Very soon I learned that I wasn't the only one in the race. The owner used all the possible venues to find the builder with the best value, and I finally won the job, outbidding eleven other builders. My quote wasn't the lowest, but it was very very low. After ten months of hard and stressful work, I realised that I didn't make any profit. However, my client was very happy, and at the end of the project, he treated me to lunch. I paid for five units without a profit; he paid for lunch. Good deal for the client.

Ringwood

3
Should I Contact the Builder First or the Architect/Draftsman?

One of the biggest mistakes to make during the building process is to get the design done before you consult with the builder.

Far too often clients approach me with fully finalised town-planning documents, working drawings, engineering drawings and energy assessments, sometimes spending in excess of $30,000 before they start looking for a builder, then they realise that their design is too ambitious for their budget. The main cause of this situation is that, regardless of the architect's/draftsman's best intentions and indisputable knowledge, they'll get paid for their drawings whether or not the project goes ahead. Builders, on the other hand, lose time every minute they speak with you about your project not being able to meet your budget expectation.

One of the first questions any good builder should ask on their first site visit, if not earlier during a phone conversation, is 'What is your budget?' or 'What budget are you hoping for?' It's much easier to work the design around the budget than the budget around the design. The biggest savings in building can be made during the design stage. Any good builder should have his own trusted architect/draftsman and engineer, and the builder should be able to give a realistic, non-obligatory, verbal cost estimate on the first site visit to make sure that everyone is on the same page. Obviously the price may vary due to circumstances at the time not known to the builder, such as town-planning requirements, exact design features, geotechnical difficulties, Bush Fire Attack Level (BAL) and similar; however, we should have a ball-park figure established by the builder quite early on.

On your first meeting with the builder, you should disclose what kind of price you're expecting. It may be completely unrealistic, and that's fine. The builder should advise you that he can't get it done for the price you're hoping for. I find that some clients are very uncomfortable about disclosing what their budget is—maybe they're afraid that the builder will overcharge them.

Good builders should also propose their own practical and cost-efficient ways of delivering the most appropriate solution.

Case Study

I was approached by clients whose architect had told them that their extension project should cost them X, and I quoted twice that amount. I didn't hear from them for a few months, and when they contacted me again, they told me that my quote was cheaper than the other two quotes they got. They considered selling the property and buying something more appropriate for their needs, but they couldn't afford anything suitable, so they asked me, 'What can we do?'

'Well,' I replied, 'let's start from the beginning and create the design to suit the budget.'

After an eight-month delay at the beginning of the Covid pandemic when the prices started to rise sharply, we ended up with reduced original drawings and a small price reduction from the original design.

4

Can I Use a Square Metre Price to Estimate the Cost of My Project?

Clients often ask me, 'What is your square-metre ratio? How much do you charge per square metre?'

This question is similar to asking how much a car costs. The answer depends on what you're looking for. Are you looking for a Kia or a Mercedes? Also, the top-of-the-range Kia can be double the price of a basic Mercedes.

The price per square metre is only valid when we compare very similar buildings. It's mainly suitable for assessing volume builders on new developments, where site costs are the same and the design is very similar. I also use square-metre comparisons when quoting clients for a new project, so I can compare them with previous projects to make sure I don't miss something and ensure steady profitability for the company. However, it only works with similar projects. A brand-new, good-quality house on sloping land with some tricky retaining walls starts at $3,500 per square metre in 2022. Volume builders on flat land can build a house with similar inclusions for less than half of this square-metre price.

Generally, the price per square metre goes down with the size, because there are quite a few fixed costs associated with each project, but documentation for tricky small extensions can be significantly higher than documentation for a large simple house …

The widest fluctuations in prices are with extensions. The most expensive are second-storey additions. To justify the cost, we should only consider them when all other options are exhausted. Ground-floor additions are obviously less expensive.

Case study

I was approached by a client who had finalised plans for adding an ensuite to his bedroom. The design (done by his architect) assumed extending the roof of the existing building and a concrete slab below with all the associated underground drainage. The whole footprint of the newly proposed bathroom was less than six square metres, but due to all the other work required, I didn't see how I could complete the project for less than $70,000 before even calculating my profit. The total cost per square metre of this project was around $15,000, but it could have been significantly less if someone consulted with the builder before the design process started.

5
Should I Pay for a Quote?

More and more builders are requesting payment for a quote. Some clients see this as outrageous and think that the builders want to rip them off. Clients should understand that the builder is not less important or knowledgeable than an architect or engineer, and nobody expects an architect or engineer to do anything for free.

We all take as a given that we can walk into a car dealership and within a short time we can walk out with the exact price of our desired car; however, it's not that straightforward with custom buildings. It's quite understandable that volume builders would be able to provide fixed quotes for their standard-range off-the-shelf house where all quantities are calculated once and then just need to be copied for each client.

It's quite different for anything custom designed. Extensions could be very tricky to quote accurately. It takes a lot of time and previous experience to get all the expenses right without underquoting and sending the company belly up or overquoting and not getting the job due to an excessive price.

Most good custom builders will advise on first meeting with the clients that they expect to be paid for a quotation, and they'll outline all design and quotation costs for the clients' consideration. It's not that those builders want to make money out of quotations (if that were the case, they would be professional estimators and not builders), it's just so they know that the client is committed. The majority of clients who pay for a quote will also go ahead with the job. If everything has already been explained to them, the final dollar figure in the quotation is probably within the range they already expected, and the quotation is done with great care and clearly defines what is included and what is not.

We at Toto Properties occasionally engage the services of an external estimator payable by the client who produces extremely accurate and detailed cost estimates up to seventy pages long. We find it extremely useful for new custom homes, where a full breakdown eliminates the possibility for misunderstandings and disputes. With extensions/renovations, however, we prefer to make the cost estimate ourselves; there are always too many hidden surprises which no estimator can predict.

6
How to Finance a Building Project

Construction projects are without a doubt one of the most expensive ventures one can take during a lifetime, and it's not always easy to obtain adequate funds for a construction. The easiest way is to use our savings. However, this option may work only for smaller projects, such as decking/pergola jobs or minor internal refurbishments.

For most construction projects, we will need to talk to some sort of financial institution. I don't recommend that you talk directly to your bank, as the person to whom you speak there works nine to five, and their wage will most likely not change if they organise your loan. Construction loans tend to be complex, and trying to get a generally unmotivated person to carry the extra burden of your loan may end up in a lengthy process full of frustration and disappointment. It's much better to talk to a mortgage broker. They're a bit like builders in that they get paid only for completed jobs, so they'll be much more motivated to get your finances in order as soon as possible.

With a financial institution involved, there are two major ways of financing the project. The easiest and most straightforward way is that you use your existing equity to back your loan. In this case, the financial institution will generally just hand you the cash without further questions, and you will pay the builder from your account as the work progresses. This type of loan is mainly used for renovations and extensions. The good thing about these loans is that they provide flexibility. We often agree with owners to do just part of a job (mainly heavy-duty structural stuff), and the owner can engage his own subcontractors to complete the project. This saves some builders' margin on the project.

When there's not enough equity available, the financial institution can lend against the building contract. The domestic construction industry in Australia is heavily regulated, and each building contract over $17,000 must be backed by home owner warranty insurance. The home owner warranty may lead you to believe that this insurance protects you, but this is only partially true; it's mainly created to protect the Australian financial industry. If a builder is unable to fulfil his contractual obligations, the home owner warranty insurance will cover the cost of completing the contractual obligations.

When a building contract is needed to secure the finances, the financial institution will carefully assess the contract and associated plans to ensure that the contract price is in line with industry standards and that the bank funds will be backed by real bricks and mortar. With unconventional building done by Toto Properties, we often disagree with bank valuers, and often lengthy explanations are needed as to where certain project costs come from. With these types of loans, the bank pays the builder directly as the work progresses according to the construction milestones defined in the contract. The owner isn't involved in the transaction, except for forwarding the builder's invoice to the financial institution. Before the final payment, the bank will usually send their valuer on site to confirm that the construction has been completed as per the contract. Some financial institutions also require a certificate of final inspection from the building surveyor.

7
The Role of the Building Surveyor

Building surveyors issue building permits. A few decades ago, there were only council surveyors, but the system was slow and inefficient. After the introduction of private building surveyors, the industry became more flexible and cost competitive. The work of building surveyors in Victoria is strictly supervised and regulated by the Victorian Building Authority (VBA).

Recently the VBA began putting a lot of pressure on building surveyors with additional requests for various documents to be included in the building permit. A lot of them are related to building–product certifications, which, in my humble opinion, should be done by manufacturers before being allowed on the market. (Remember the defective cladding saga?) However, the VBA is just another bureaucratic institution unconcerned about anybody's convenience, blindly following the law and shifting responsibility down the chain. Building surveyors simply shift these requests onto the builders' and homeowners' shoulders.

Most good builders will have a preferred building surveyor whom they normally use; however, the building surveyor does need to be appointed by the client. Normally we get our clients to sign the application form for our surveyor.

We prefer to use the smallest surveying company possible. The best is a 'one-man band' where the same person issues the building permit and conducts all site inspections. With our type of complex buildings, things rarely work out exactly as planned, and often we need last-minute variations to existing plans. With a surveyor familiar with the project, it's much easier to navigate all the compliance requirements.

Most building surveyors just work in offices and issue building permits. For site inspections they appoint independent building inspectors, whose role is not to check if something is built good or bad, but strictly to check if something is built in compliance with the approved plans or not. Inspectors on site may verbally agree that a deviation from the plan improved the building quality, but they aren't authorised to approve it and will seek amendments of the plans.

There are only around 400 building surveyors in Victoria, and everyone is very busy. Building permit applications are getting slower and slower to be approved.

Case study

A few years ago, we started building a second-storey addition where the client organised all the documentation himself, including appointing a large surveying company. After we started the construction and opened a large section of the roof on a house where the owner still lived during the works, we discovered several discrepancies (quite common with extensions). The large timber beam specified by the client's engineers didn't fit in the space provided. So as not to lose any time, I got our own engineer to specify a smaller steel alternative. Everything was done within hours, and the next morning I had the required steel beam on site, and we installed it within the same day. We were in a rush to cover and enclose the building to make the living conditions inside the tarp-covered house a bit more human.

However, when the frame was completed, the inspector (appointed by the large surveying company) refused to accept my engineer's beam and requested that the original engineers, who provided the engineering for the whole project, should approve it. It took three weeks to get somebody from this engineering company (again, a large company) to come on site and confirm the beam specified by my engineer. They also charged a fee for this, and then it took another week for the large surveying company to amend the building permit (and charge another fee).

So this whole saga, with all its associated stress and costs, took nearly a month during a Melbourne winter. The moral of the story is: make sure you engage surveyors, designers and architects with maximum responsiveness; people who return emails within twenty-four hours or earlier and are available on the phone most of the time. Responsive Building Surveyor is very important in any building project by providing relevant advice and ensure compliance with Australian Standards.

8

The Difference Between Planning Permits & Building Permits

Clients often confuse these two documents. We need a building permit for almost all construction activities and, in most cases, people use private building surveyors to issue a building permit (we can also engage a council building surveyor, but they tend to be less responsive). A building permit is usually issued within weeks (assuming that all the requested documentation is provided to the building surveyor). It has become a more common practice by private building surveyors to ask the builder/client to provide a written statement from the council that a planning permit isn't needed before they issue a building permit. This is mainly due to the complexity of the language associated with descriptions in town planning overlays, which makes clear interpretations very difficult, even for surveyors otherwise skilled with planning jargon.

A planning permit, however, can be only issued by a council planning department. There is no specific rule as to when a planning permit is needed; it all depends on what overlays are applicable on your land. It may be related to removal of vegetation, site coverage, subdivision to smaller lots or countless other situations. Planning permits can take a few months to a few years for more complex projects. For simple projects there are so-called Vic Smart applications, which should be resolved within fourteen days. In most cases it's double this time, but still faster than the standard process. You should try to avoid a planning permit if possible. See the case study below.

Case study

We were engaged to build a living room extension with a small deck in the Yarra Ranges Council area. Our surveyor asked for council confirmation that a planning permit wasn't needed, and the council replied that in the Yarra Ranges Council area, a planning permit was needed for decking on any site with a slope of more than twenty degrees. So that was our trigger for getting a planning permit. To avoid the lengthy planning-permit process, we substituted decking with concrete paving.

9

Disputes

Nobody likes to argue, and the best way to avoid disputes is to have a clear understanding of what our rights and obligations are under the building contract. Good builders should take the time to educate their clients about how the building process will go and what is included and not included in the agreed scope of works.

The client should ask whenever they have any uncertainty about any matter in the building contract or during construction. There is no such thing as a stupid question, and the builder should be able to answer and explain in clear language.

I strongly suggest that all communication goes via emails, or when there is a verbal communication and an agreement is reached, that parties confirm the agreement via email. It may be as simple as: 'Dear Mr Smith, as per our conversation earlier today, we agreed about xyz. Please confirm by replying to this email.' Or the agreement could be more formal in the shape of variation forms detailing the scope and price of variation.

When a dispute arises between the client and the builder, the matter can be referred to Domestic Building Dispute Resolution Victoria (DBDRV) by any party. This is a free service from the Victorian government that assists parties to reach an agreement. Only if parties fail to reach an agreement in DBDRV can the dispute be referred to the Victorian Civil and Administrative Tribunal (VCAT).

Disputes between builders and clients should be avoided whenever possible with clear and open communication. When an agreement can't be reached and the matter ends up in court, there is, in the end, usually only one clear winner: the lawyers.

10
Should I Engage an Independent Building Inspector?

Every building project with a building permit has a building surveyor who checks the building project during its progress. However, the role of building surveyor is not that much about the quality of the building, but rather legality and whether the minimum standard requirements are met.

Good builders should have good building practice systems in place to ensure that the relevant standard requirements and good workmanship are met. No independent inspector is a substitute for bad workmanship and unprofessional subcontractors.

For peace of mind, however, it may be a good idea to engage an independent inspector. It will make the builder more conscious of building quality, and perhaps they'll pay more attention to details. Regardless of the builder's best intentions, some items may be overlooked, and the inspector can pick them up so they can be rectified.

There are, however, a few instances where a 'dedicated' building inspector can create more harm than good. Inspectors might, in their report, describe certain defects and cite the relevant standard next to it that describes the defect. However, one of the 'defects' we came across in this situation was a 'cold joint' in concrete. When a concrete slab is poured, usually concreters pour the trenches first and then the top 100 mm of the slab. When the formwork is removed, there may be a visible line between the trenches and the top of the slab. This line is called a 'cold joint', and it could be a serious problem in very complex structures, such as suspension bridges; however, it's quite irrelevant with domestic house slabs. That inspector made an already anxious client very worried, and I needed to get an independent engineering report to calm down the client. This is the kind of thing that can happen when an inspector applies standards created for one kind of building to another kind.

11
Types of Building Projects

Decking

Decking is a widespread, popular feature of Australian homes. Since outdoor structures must be constructed from materials suitable for exposure to the elements, decking frames are most commonly made of H3 treated pine, which is suitable for exterior above-ground use. For the in-ground parts, we have to use concrete, steel or durable timber species, such as cyprus, red gum, merbau or H4 treated pine. In high bushfire areas (BAL29 and above), we have to fully enclose the treated-pine frame (gaps up to 3 mm are permitted) or use a bushfire-resistant species of timber or steel.

The decking boards themselves can be made from a wide range of timber species. The cheapest is H3 treated pine; probably the most widespread is merbau, which comes in widths of 70 mm, 90 mm and 140 mm; spotted gum is also popular; blackbutt and ironbark are less common, mainly due to limited availability and the associated price. We have also used laminated bamboo, which was easy to lay and has performed quite well over the ten-year period since installation. Recently, various deckings made of recycled plastic have come onto the market. These have gained some popularity due to their superior visual appearance and no need for oiling or other maintenance. The main drawback of these products is the huge expansion rate that comes with temperature changes, and so the boards need to be laid in a specific way to eliminate huge gaps between the boards. The other drawback is that nobody knows how they will look fifteen years from now, and an already recycled plastic product may be hard to recycle again.

Decking boards can be fixed to the supporting frame in different ways. In use are specially designed dome-head nails made either from galvanised steel or stainless steel, but probably the best option is to fix the decking directly down with stainless-steel screws. There are a few self-drilling products on the market, but nothing beats a pedantic carpenter carefully predrilling the hole in the boards for every single screw. The other option is to screw the decking from the side with specially designed screws or use grooved decking boards and fix it down with specially designed brackets.

Concealed fixing method on merbau decking

Excavations

Most new builds, extensions, and landscaping will involve some sort of excavation. It may be just small footings for decking, potentially dug by hand, or a large site cut in rocky terrain on sloping land that would involve large excavators and several trucks with trailers for disposal of the excavated material.

It's crucial to get as much information as possible about the terrain before excavation starts. For new builds in extensions, a building permit will require a geotechnical report—in building jargon known as a 'soil test'. This gives the builder a good idea about what they're dealing with deep underground. Valuable information can also be obtained from the Dial Before You Dig service. Some information can also be gotten from a 'land slip assessment', a specialised geotechnical report required on most steep sites within the Yarra Ranges Council.

The local water authority will also have very reliable and accurate diagrams about underground sewer lines, which are very valuable to have during footing excavations for extensions. In my extensive experience of extension buildings, I hardly remember any project where we didn't encounter any sewer or stormwater pipe, which must then be promptly diverted. When negotiating with a builder about a proposed extension, make sure that potential damage of underground services is included in the total contract price and that the builder has the resources to fix it promptly if an accident happens. There are no records or diagrams for most stormwater pipes in most backyards, and damage of the pipes is, in most cases, inevitable and must be dealt with before the next rain to avoid excessive site saturation with stormwater.

With large site cuts, it's very difficult to estimate the exact amount of soil to be taken away and the associated costs. However, any reputable builder should give you a fixed price for the whole project, regardless of uncertainty. Most unexpected costs arise from contaminated soils. We've discovered many nasty surprises buried in backyards, including asbestos. Luckily, no dead bodies, so far …

Large amounts of clean fill, such as clay without top soil, can be in many cases be disposed of without a dumping fee at different sites all around Melbourne where they are needed for site stabilisation, levelling and similar. Most good excavation businesses will also have established contacts for soil disposal. There is also a [Facebook group where you can post your request for soil needed or soil to be disposed of](#).

Concreting

Concrete is one of the most widespread materials used in the construction industry. Home owners will generally engage concreters for new driveways, landings, steps, cross overs, paths and house slabs—in the case of owner builders.

Concreters range from small one-man bands suitable for very small jobs to very skilled large teams who normally deal with house slabs or similar larger projects. Concrete as a building material allows for many different finishes, such as:

Coloured concrete

This is used for driveways, walkways and similar. It should be laid on a bed of crushed rock and be reinforced to minimise cracking. Coloured concrete has an oxide pigment mixed into the concrete mix and should be sealed with a concrete sealer to enhance the colour. The sealer does fade away after a few years and should be reapplied to keep the original shiny appearance.

Plain grey concrete

This is the most basic form of concrete and is usually smooth trowelled in case of house slabs or rough trowelled in case of driveways, walkways and similar. It should be laid on a bed of crushed rock and reinforced with steel for larger areas to minimise cracking.

Exposed aggregate concrete

This is one of the most complex to install and requires a concreter with good skill to get the desirable outcome. The client chooses their desired mix of texture and colour from what is available at the nearest concrete plant where they provide exposed aggregate concrete. After the concrete has been laid to the desired area and height, it gets sprayed with a chemical which prevents the upper layer of the concrete hardening. The next day the concrete is washed off with a high-pressure water jet to expose the beautiful structure. Exposed aggregate concrete should get sealed immediately after being washed.

Burnished concrete

This is normally plain-grey concrete trowelled to high smoothness with mechanical trowels (helicopters). Some helicopters have Teflon blades to achieve an extreme level of smoothness. Burnished concrete is most common in large commercial projects (most Bunnings stores have burnished concrete floors). However, recently it has become popular in domestic applications as a more cost-effective alternative to polished concrete.

Polished concrete

This is one of the most complex kinds of concrete to install and finish. It may be just plain-grey concrete or any possible colour mix, and when laid it can be sprayed with pebbles or any type of small rocks of different colours and shapes. It's very difficult to achieve consistency, and the concreter should educate the client about the expected imperfections in the final product. The polishing process itself can be done just with rough grinding and sealing the surface with polyurethane sealant. However, that's the cheap way, and the concrete sealer will become yellowish in colour as time passes. The best way is to get a very smooth finish, which doesn't require any sealant and will provide a lifelong finish to the floor. Concreters achieve this level of smoothness by using mechanical 'helicopters' with Teflon blades, fast spinning them over concrete a few hours after it's laid. You can see these kinds of finishes in warehouses such as Bunnings or similar.

Polished concrete around swimming pools should be acid-etched to avoid them being slippery.

Despite concrete's widespread use, due to its durability and practicality, there are a few drawbacks. First, the production of concrete is an extremely high-carbon emission process. Second, on the more aesthetic side, there are two types of concrete: the concrete which has cracked, and the concrete which will crack. Cracking of concrete by itself isn't a defect if it's within the tolerances described in the Guide to Standards and Tolerances, and there are different ways to minimise cracking. The most common and obvious is to install steel reinforcement in the concrete; the other is to make control joints at the weak points—they can be cut in cured concrete or trowelled in during the concrete pour.

Brickwork

Brickwork is normally part of larger building projects. However, a homeowner may engage only bricklayers for various projects.

One of the most common independent bricklaying projects is building a front fence. With this project, you should pay a lot of attention to what is allowed under your local council regulations and be sure to establish the exact line of your front boundary. If the front boundary isn't yet exactly determined, it's best to engage a licensed land surveyor.

Before brickwork on the front boundary starts, you'll need foundations with an appropriate depth and width of footing plus associated steel reinforcement. Attention needs to be paid during the excavation of the front footing to not damage the existing services that run underground to your property. Telecommunication services can be quite shallow. Gas and electrical services should be a minimum of 600 mm deep, but don't take my word for it; sometimes they run shallower. Water supply may be at any depth.

Before any digging, you should get all available information on Dial Before You Dig at https://www.1100.com.au/ However, not all information is there, and sometimes, before the excavator can be engaged, careful hand excavation is needed until all services are located.

Sometimes all that's required is to patch up existing damaged brickwork or alter it as desired. It's quite an art to get old brickwork patched up without the patch being noticeable. First you need to source the matching bricks. Depending on the age of the existing brickwork, the best way is usually to visit the nearest new brick supplier. We mostly use [Melbourne Brick](). They have an expert who comes on site to assess existing brickwork and suggests the closest match. The other option is to visit brick recycling companies. We use [Beaver Bricks](); they have a wide range of old bricks and, with a bit of luck, you can find a perfect match.

Beautiful example of newly laid recycled bricks

The other important visual element in brickwork is mortar. Mortar can be done in different ways: finished flush with the face of the bricks or rolled in. In older projects it was recessed about 10 mm inside the face of the brickwork. The trickiest of all is to match the mortar colour, as colour depends mainly on the type of sand used in the original mix as well as the type of cement. Also, colour changes as the mortar dries, so what may seem like a perfectly matching mix may look quite different a few days later.

A good bricklayer should inform you about the possible imperfections, and there is no guarantee of a 100% perfect match, however skilled the bricklayer, but a bit of luck can lead to repairs that looks near perfect and impossible to spot for the average observer.

Landscaping

Good landscaping can make a massive difference in the appearance of the home. Landscaping is mainly about surfaces and plants around the buildings; however, it can get quite complex and intricate when large rocks are introduced, sometimes around swimming pools or ponds with potential streams of water and incorporated on decking with irregular shapes on different elevations. Landscapers also deal with retaining walls.

Good landscapers are quite hard to find and are usually very busy.

Pergolas

Pergolas are considered any outdoor areas covered with a roof and attached to the house. If the structure is not attached to the house, we call it a gazebo.

We do need building permits for covered pergolas. Only unroofed pergolas with an area of less than 20 square metres are exempt.

There are many different types of pergolas, from simple structures covered with polycarbonate roof sheets to very sophisticated structures with ceilings, integrated downlights, ceiling fans and even in-ceiling built-in speakers. Accordingly, the price can vary dramatically.

All roofed pergolas must have their own gutters with connections to a legal point of discharge on your property. Only qualified and registered roof plumbers can install metal or polycarbonate roof sheets on a pergola with all its associated guttering and downpipes.

In regard to Victorian regulations, it's legal for anyone to lay a tiled roof on any appropriate framed structure. There is no legal requirement for any kind of licensing or work experience. It is, however, an offence if anyone not registered with the Victorian Building Authority installs a metal roof sheet or even a polycarbonate roof sheet.

The theme of this job was "Thinking out of square" with curved decking and lining cyprus posts.

Bathroom or laundry renovation

Bathroom and laundries are wet areas of the house, and water has a very destructive and damaging force on buildings. Even when bathrooms are a quality build and well maintained, we expect them to be in need of renovation in about twenty years.

There are no shortcuts when dealing with bathrooms and laundries. The only real way to do it is to strip everything out of the room, including plaster or at least most of the plaster, and carefully assess any potential water damage to the timber framing. Special attention is to be paid to the floor and junctions between the wall and floor.

When the bathroom is cleared of all old fixtures, tiles and plaster, the plumber can run new piping, including hot and cold water and waste-water pipes. At this point, to make sure the connections are in the right spot, it's important that the plumber knows the exact type of toilet you will use as well as shower mixer, shower rail and vanity taps.

If a wall-hung vanity unit is required, the carpenter

will have to consider this and install enough hard-fixing points in the wall to deal with the weight of the vanity unit. The same consideration must be done if you plan to hang a washing machine or dryer on the wall of the laundry. Placement of toilet-roll holders and towel holders will also need to be considered at this point.

After the plumber, an electrician can install provisions for the proposed power points, lights, exhaust fans, heated towel rails and automated toilets—if you plan to install one. Careful planning consideration is needed for power points around vanity units, as they can't be closer than 150 mm from the edge of the vanity bowl and need to be 400 mm above. In small and constrained bathrooms, this could be quite an issue, and a lot of careful planning is needed to achieve compliance with regulations.

When all installations are in place, there is a need for plastering. Only a water-resistant and approved plasterboard or fibre-cement product can be used for lining bathroom walls, and floors need to be made either of 20 mm compressed fibre-cement sheets or lined with 6 mm fibre-cement sheets over structural timber flooring. If a tiled shower base is proposed, there has to be provision for structurally sound cement screeding, which should be not thinner than 20 mm or, alternatively, an off-the-shelf, ready-made shower bed can be installed.

The waterproofing happens after all the floor and wall lining has been installed. This is the single most often misunderstood step and the point of many failures.

Australian Standard AS3740 deals with bathroom waterproofing and should be strictly followed, including manufacturer installation instructions.

After the waterproofing is installed and cured as per manufacturer instructions, it's time for tilers. They usually start with the tiled shower bed (if there is one) and work all the floors before starting the walls. When all the tiles are laid, they apply grout between them. However, there should be no grout on the wall–floor junction or wall–wall junctions. These junctions should have flexible, sanitary-grade, coloured silicone sealant to allow for expansion of different surfaces and minimise water penetration between the tiles.

When the tiles are done, the carpenters or cabinetmakers can install the vanity units, and the plumber can install the toilet, taps and bowls. This is also the time for the electrician to fit all power points and switches. Then the glazier installs the shower screens and mirrors, and a corker seals all the gaps.

Structural modifications

Our way of life is constantly changing, and as our lifestyle changes, so do our needs for living spaces. Forty or fifty years ago, it was normal to use one room for cooking and eating our meals and another room for family gatherings and watching TV. Today we prefer these two rooms joined in what we call open-plan living.

To achieve open-plan living in old houses, we need to remove a wall or a few walls to create a large open area. This inevitably changes the house's structural integrity and the way it was designed. Clients often refer to 'load-bearing walls' or 'structural walls', but the truth is that even if a particular wall doesn't support the load above it, it's still part of the existing house structure that acts as a brace for racking forces. Racking forces are forces acting on a house in a horizontal way, such as wind and earthquakes.

A good builder should be able to determine what is needed for a particular structural modification. However, they will need a structural engineer to specify beams, bracing and connections for any wall removal. Transferring a load from a wall to a beam will create additional forces on each side of the beam, and this will, in most cases, need additional support on either side and sometimes footing reinforcement. It may be relatively easy to provide additional footing support if the house is built on stumps. Usually this is done by opening the floor and excavating an additional footing under the house. If the house is on a concrete slab and the engineer specifies footing reinforcement, it's a much bigger and more complex job to provide the desired support for the beam.

Beams can be steel or timber. Timber beams can be solid timber or glue-laminated timber or LVL which stands for laminated veneer lumber. LVL is very popular due to a wide range of availability of sizes and lengths and exact engineering tables specifying load-bearing ability. In most cases they also have some degree of termite protection.

It may seem simple to remove a wall or a few walls and replace them with beams, but much more is involved. Almost all walls have live electrical wires running through them and sometimes water and gas pipes, which need to be dealt with. In the ceiling above the walls, we will find evaporative cooling ducts and ducted heating ducts, ducted heating heaters with associated gas pipes and electrical supply, and old gravity-feed water heaters—which most often have been disconnected decades ago, but nobody took them out of the roof space. And, yes, we do find many dead possums and rats.

Most structural modifications will need a building permit.

Complex structural modification/
extension for project In Upwey

Extensions

When there is not enough room in the house due to an additional family member or other circumstances, we first try to see if the family's needs can be met by simply rearranging internal spaces; for example, dividing one large bedroom into two small ones. In most cases, however, that's rarely an option, and we need to increase the external perimeter of the house. If that's also not possible due to lack of available room on the land, then, as the last and most expensive resort, we add a second storey on top of the existing house.

Extensions are very complex building projects, and the price per square metre will almost always be much higher than for a brand-new home. The large price hardly ever comes from the cost of any single item in this kind of construction; rather, the final figure is usually composed out of hundreds of small items and steps. However, a costly roof line could potentially be avoided. Incorporating the existing roof line over the new extension usually means a lot of work on the existing roof as well as on the new roof. When the client is on a tight budget, we suggest giving the extension a flat roof; that minimises the work on the existing roof and speeds up the process.

When designing an extension, we are, most often, aiming for the same appearance as the existing building. However, sometimes designers intentionally add a contemporary-looking addition to an old-fashioned house and, if designed properly, it can look very good.

When building an extension, there is almost always also some work to be done on the existing house. Setting the floor level of the proposed addition requires careful consideration, as do the floor coverings, to ensure a smooth and seamless transition from the old to the new part of the extended house. During the construction, there will, almost always, be some interruptions of the existing underground or overhead services, so careful consideration, planning and research is needed to locate the existing services and decide how to deal with them.

Even the best design and designer can't predict everything needed in one extension. When work starts, we often encounter surprises, but a good, experienced builder should be able to make allowances for most of the possible scenarios.

Volume builders

Volume builders are normally found in the outer suburbs on new land developments. Generally they'll have their show houses near large developments, and they can be an extremely cost-efficient way to get a new home. They will have their home designs ready with all associated pricing and inclusions, and often they'll offer land and home packages with very low deposits.

Due to the volume of their turnover, they're able to obtain very good prices from their suppliers and subcontractors. Fixed designs also mean that their standard homes can be built without intensive supervision, and one site manager can manage ten or more building sites simultaneously, making the process more cost efficient.

Volume builders also know exactly, with great precision, how much of each material will go into individual homes, making them able to work on a very slim margin. Unfortunately, slim margins and great competition between volume builders mean that they quite often fail and go bankrupt, leaving numerus clients out of pocket and making newspaper headlines.

The other downside of volume builders is that they're quite inflexible with changes to their set designs. All their subcontractors are very familiar with the designs, and any changes must be documented and plans changed and forwarded to site supervisors and subcontractors. All this makes any change a costly exercise.

Volume builders are a good and cost-efficient way for first home owners to get their first home. The downside is that they most often operate in outer suburbs that don't have very well-developed infrastructure such as schools, hospitals and jobs.

Custom homes

A lot of effort goes into each custom home. Architects and designers work with clients to produce beautiful plans, which remain just that—plans—if the builder isn't involved early on.

The builder is the only person in the design–construction project who gets paid only if the construction goes ahead. For that reason, the builder will need to make sure they meet the client's budget expectation and capabilities. One major cost-related parameter is, obviously, the size, so very early on the size of the proposed building will need to be determined. In most cases clients realise early on that fourteen bedrooms, ten bathrooms, four living areas and an underground basketball court will be a bit over their available budget, so we cut back their dream design to suit more everyday needs.

The level of finishes and inclusions is another cost-related parameter. Surprisingly, we can get quite extravagant-looking finishes that don't break the budget by using off-the-shelf solutions and products. Prices tend to skyrocket when a lot of custom-made details are specified, as these consume a lot of time from highly skilled/paid trades.

Another factor affecting the budget is the Bush Fire

Attack Level, known as the BAL rating. A high bushfire rating could significantly affect the price. So the bushfire rating of your site should be determined very early on in the design process.

It's very likely that custom homes will be on sloping sites, and the degree of slope and general accessibility will affect the design and construction cost significantly. Difficult excavation due to rocky terrain and the necessity of retaining walls can contribute significantly to the overall cost.

An engineer will need to be consulted soon after the preliminary drawings are completed and confirmed by all parties—architect, builder and owner. Engineers, however, do tend to specify standard solutions, which they just copy and paste into the engineering drawings. Architects are mostly unaware of the cost implications of such copy-and-paste structural design—why would they care when they'll get paid regardless of whether the construction will ever begin? Experienced builders should, at this point, suggest/require alternative solutions from the engineer. The most obvious example is the use of core-filled blockwork or core-filled double brickwork as retaining walls. It's very labour intensive to bring concrete blocks on site, lay them up, reinforce them with steel, then core fill them with structural grout and finally waterproof the finished product. Much faster and more cost efficient is to use core-filled PVC panels, which are much faster to install, cheaper and don't require waterproofing. We use [AFS formwork](#).

For a custom home, it's a good idea to engage an *experienced* interior designer. I say *experienced* because it's important that suggested finishes aren't just taken from Pinterest or Instagram, but are exactly what the plans specify, with the supplier and price attached.

It is quite common that local council regulations require a planning permit for a custom home, and this should be determined very early on and the required application lodged with the council. Usually no major design work is done during the planning-permit waiting time due to the risk that the council may request a major change that requires a significant overhaul of the existing design. When a planning permit (where needed) is granted, there are no major legal obstacles for the project to go ahead.

The final version of the working and engineering drawings can be completed, and we should already have the BAL report and the geotechnical report (also known as the 'soil test' in construction jargon). An energy performance assessment will need to be done and, if building on sloping land, a landslip assessment may also be required. We will need a legal point of discharge from the council and, if that's not available, they'll request a stormwater-discharge system done by a civil engineer. Surveyors will also ask if the property is serviced by a mains sewer and, if it isn't, the council sanitary department will specify an on site septic system, which may be an additional and quite-costly item.

Custom home built in Belgrave

Concrete slab or stumps?

There is no clear-cut answer to the question of whether to build a home on a concrete slab or stumps. It all depends on each particular site and the shape of the proposed building.

Generally, concrete slabs are more suitable for flat land with a consistent soil profile. There is also some thermal performance benefit. Soil at a depth of one metre is around 14°C in the middle of a Melbourne winter. If we put a concrete slab on it, this energy helps to warm the house. Two identical houses, one on a slab and one on stumps, will have significant difference in thermal performance due to heat from the ground.

The downside of a concrete slab is that it requires a

lot of preparation work beforehand. All the underground sewer, stormwater pipes and electrical supply need to be organised before the slab is poured. It's not uncommon for concreters to break sewer pipes during preparation works, and if this isn't rectified immediately, it could be a big and very expensive job when the house is completed.

A good builder should organise a pipe inspection with a plumbing camera to avoid later problems. All slab penetrations, such as pipes, should also get treated by a termite specialist to avoid potential infestation. Also needed is great precision in positioning the pipes. It's extremely difficult if, after the concrete is poured, we discover that we have a toilet pipe in the middle of the living room. Concrete slabs are also an extremely carbon-intensive structure.

Stumps, on the other hand, offer more flexibility in setting different floor levels in the same house. All plumbing can be done at a later date when the frame is already erected and positions exactly determined.

The most common stump material is concrete. However, timber stumps are still in use, and they could have a long lifespan if there's good drainage. We prefer to use electro-galvanised steel posts with additional protective coating, as they're much easier to handle than concrete stumps and offer a greater lifespan than timber stumps.

Steel stumps for house on sloping land in Belgrave

Multi units

Many people recognise that it's possible to make a great profit by subdividing their land into multiple smaller lots and building individual units on it. These projects vary in size from putting a single unit or townhouse on the back of an existing house up to twelve or more units on a previously single piece of land.

The subdivision process is lengthy and complex. Financial viability often depends on how many units one can build on certain land. Designers have different levels of skill and experience, and it's well worth talking to different designers to get their opinion about how many units can be built on your land. This can make the difference between making money or making a loss.

A good example of the difference between a good and bad designer is the project at number six Bedford Rd, Ringwood. If you drive past, you'll see a five-unit development on only 700 square metres of land. You see that the side walls are made from bricks, but the front wall is smooth sheet cladding. This is because the standard brick-veneer wall is 240 mm wide, whereas a sheet-cladded wall is only 110 mm wide; this 130 mm difference meant that the designer was able to squeeze five units on site instead of four, which made a big financial difference for the owner.

Every subdivision project needs to be approved by the council, and they won't necessarily approve a designer's opinion. Countless conditions need to be met before gaining council approval. Every council has its own rules, and every land has different overlays, so even within the same council, there may be vastly different conditions to meet before final approval is granted.

Council will not only dictate the height and shape of units but also common services. Plans need to be approved for the driveway, complex stormwater systems and even landscaping with an exact schedule of every plant to be planted and where.

The approval process for simple projects may be resolved in six months or even less, but more often than not, we should allow twelve months or more before the project is ready for construction.

When building three or more units on site, most councils will also require payment of an open-space contribution, which is a kind of council tax on new developments. This is a significant amount of money and should be considered when calculating the financial feasibility of the project.

Multi-unit projects attract a lot of builders due to the significant amount of money involved. However, where there is a lot of money, there is a lot of competition, and many builders get into such projects with very small margins and so the rate of bankruptcies within multi-unit builders is very high. It can be very painful for an investor to have a builder go bankrupt in the middle of their project. It will be difficult to get a new builder to complete the job, and the new builder will charge significantly more than the previous builder. There are many cases where a builder entered into a new multi-unit contract very cheaply, just to get the job, because he lost money on a previous job and is desperate for some fresh cashflow. However, this cycle can be repeated only two or three times before the builder is met with reality and finally goes bankrupt.

Investors should be very wary about multi-unit builders offering very low prices. If anything seems to be too good to be true, it probably is. More experienced investors are well aware of this, and once when I was in negotiation for an eight-apartment building in Mentone, the owner, an experienced investor with many past projects, told me, 'I can't afford a builder who won't make any profit on my project.' Very wise words.

12
Energy Efficiency

Yesss! Finally someone realised that being energy efficient may be a good thing in Australia. The 'energy efficiency' idea is starting to gain some popularity, mainly due to influence from overseas, particularly Europe.

The coldest winter I ever experienced was in 2000 when I first visited Australia. I was staying in my aunt's house in suburban Melbourne in a house built in the early '80s. There was no insulation of any type in any part of the building; it had single-glazed windows, and the only form of heating was a gas heater in the living room. If the outside temperature on cold winter nights was three or four degrees, that was the temperature inside the bedroom—much the same as we expect from a good-performing refrigerator. That was a bit of a shock for me, coming from Slovenia. Despite a much weaker economy, I never lived in a bedroom there that didn't have some form of heating installed as part of the original design or at least retrofitted.

The medical community today agrees that the high rate of asthma in Australia correlates with the amount of cold air we breathe during long winter nights. Another very sad statistic is that there are more deaths from hypothermia in South Australia alone than in Norway; most deaths in Norway result from young-adult males under the influence of alcohol, whereas deaths in South Australia are mainly elderly people who can't afford the cost of heating.

To counteract the cold, Australian builders in the '70s and '80s started to introduce gas-ducted heating. This is arguably the worst possible form of heating someone can invent. There is no clear evidence yet if there is more health damage from cold air or from allergens and dust being constantly recirculated through our rooms via ducted heating. Adding to the problem is the inherent inefficiency of the system, being hot air forced through poorly insulated pipes with many leaks. Luckily, the rising cost of gas is slowly but surely pushing ducted systems out of the market.

Old habits die slowly, though. My children are in a recently opened childcare facility with all the latest design and equipment. The state premier attended the opening ceremony, highlighting the latest 'green design'. This childcare facility is equipped with a wide array of solar panels, has a large battery bank and an impressive heat pump array, providing hot water for heating and sanitary use. In Europe and North America, it would be the most common and sensible solution to direct this abundance of free hot water through pipes in the concrete floor for heating, but not here. In our childcare facility, it's directed to the grated radiators in the ceiling and forced down via fans—just to make sure there is a good exchange of dust and the concrete floor is kept cold. Yes, snorty kids are really cute … Welcome in the country of Ugg boots. Do you get my frustration?

Energy efficiency became popular in Europe for three main reasons: high energy cost, much colder climate, and government initiatives. None of those exist in any meaningful sense in Australia, so there is no real significant economic push to build more efficient homes. The fact that energy-efficient homes generally provide a much better feel and overall living condition is largely unknown and/or ignored. We still prefer a stone benchtop from Italy over a warm floor.

My twin boys at our home through an infra-red camera. Orange stripes indicate the pipes of warm water running under the floor, and 25.1 in the centre of the picture indicates the floor temperature

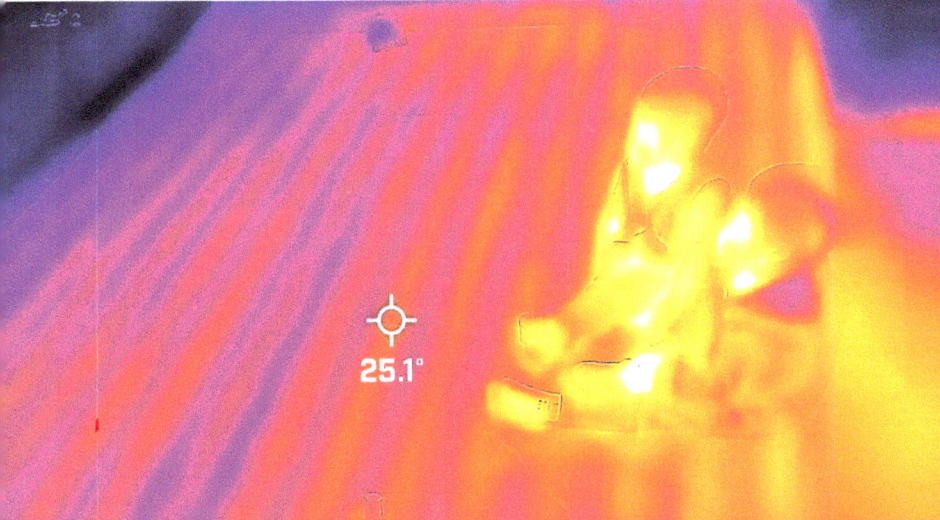

To get a good energy-efficient home, numerous factors need to be considered, but the two most important components are: first, get as much free energy as possible through solar panels and good orientation to enable winter sun to penetrate the building; second, stop the energy in the building from leaking out by using good insulation, sealing and good-performing windows.

Good-performing windows are airtight even when there's a pressure difference between indoor and outdoor. Wind blowing from one direction creates an area of low air pressure on the opposite side of a building and, where the windows aren't airtight, this literally sucks warm air from inside the house. The second component of good-performing windows is low temperature conductivity through the window frames. If window frames are made from aluminium, they should be thermally broken, meaning that the middle part is made of PVC. One of the best-performing frames are 100% PVC—however, it's not possible to use these where high-bushfire resistance is required. The last window component is glass. The glass can be single-, double- or even triple-glazed, and can be treated with invisible metallic oxides that reflect heat back into the building. Good single-glazed PVC windows may perform better than low-range aluminium double-glazed ones.

The other, often-ignored, aspect of gaining good energy efficiency is how much attention and care is put into the installation of insulation, windows and doors and other wall/ceiling/floor penetrations, and ensuring that all gaps are sealed with polyurethane foam or a similar product. It's useless to put in expensive windows and abundant insulation if all the elements are not installed properly, following manufacturer recommendations and good workmanship.

Insulation installers can often be not particularly pedantic about their job, mainly because soon after they're finished, plaster will cover the insulation and then there is no way to visually inspect their job. To solve this problem, I use a small thermal camera attached to my iPhone which clearly shows thermal gaps if there's faulty or missing insulation in the walls or ceiling. When installers are aware that I'll be able to inspect their job at a later date, they take much more care.

Missing insulation in part of the ceiling is well visible with an infra-red camera

Hydronic heating

Underfloor hydronic heating is by far my most favourite form of keeping warm. It's silent, has no airflow or emissions and feels heavenly. What's better than waking every morning and walking bare foot to the kitchen to make my morning cuppa on warm tiles, feeling the gentle heat from the floor? Even before the morning coffee, I'm forcibly reminded by this simple pleasure that life is good. It helps me to try to ignore Melbourne weather.

Hydronic heating works by pumping warm water from a heat source, which may be a heat pump, gas burner, wood burner, oil burner or in some cases thermal water from underground. (An excellent example of this is in the [Mornington Peninsular Hot Spring and Spa](#) where they heat their concrete floor with thermal water.)

Pipes could run to wall panels, known as radiators, or be cased in the concrete slab. They can also be installed in houses on stumps and retrofitted in the floor of existing houses.

Below is a photo of an excellent example of retrofitting hydronic heating. This is in my own thirty-year-old house during extensive renovations. This particular floor was later covered with carpet.

Retrofitted hydronic floor heating

Moisture management

Life is dependent on water, and wherever there is water, there is life. However, it works the opposite way as well, wherever there is life, there is water. Our life and living activities in our homes generate water. The most obvious is taking a shower or cooking when we can immediately detect a large amount of steam floating in the air and creating tiny droplets on any surface; the colder the surface, the more steam sticks to it.

Most of our shower/cooking steam is, or should be, extracted via exhaust fans and rangehoods, but that's not always perfect extraction, and there will be always more moisture inside the house than outside. In summer time when windows and doors are often wide open, that's not a problem. In winter, however, when we try to preserve the heat in the home and keep windows and doors shut, the level of indoor moisture rises significantly. All things in nature aim for equilibrium, and moisture from inside the house is drawn outside through walls, ceilings and floors, mainly through tiny gaps, but also through solid surfaces such as walls. Most materials have some degree of vapour permeability. In most cases that's not a problem (in Melbourne). However, when the amount of internal humidity is too great, and the difference between the outdoor and indoor temperature is significant, then the invisible vapour starts condensing inside the walls. Tiny droplets start to form, then droplets join and create small streams on any surface they hit. This water can lead to problems: one is causing potential structural issues by encouraging wood rot, and the other, more often encountered, is providing a breeding ground for mould that could be harmful to our health.

In building physics we refer to the 'dew point'—the point when water vapor condenses and changes from a vapor to a liquid. Have you ever noticed steam coming from your mouth in winter? Why doesn't that happen in summer when we exhale exactly the same air composed of the same gases and with the same amount of moisture? The reason is the dew point. The concentration of water in the form of gas that we exhale only becomes visible (condenses) when the ambient temperature is around five degrees or lower. If our bodies worked on eighty or one hundred degrees, then we would see the steam from our mouth even at room temperature, the same way as we see the steam rising from a pot cooking pasta.

Understanding the dew point helps us select materials by determining their water permeability so we can avoid creating dew points inside the walls, along with their related moisture problems.

As we aim to build better and more-insulated homes, it's important to carefully consider moisture management. The problem of providing fresh air in tightly insulated homes can be efficiently mitigated through ventilation systems that use a heat recuperation technique. Most European/North American energy-efficient homes would have a heat recuperation system in place to take heat energy from moist, stale, indoor air and replace it with fresh, cold, outdoor air in such a way as to minimise overall heat loss.

However, significant problems arising from air moisture are not present in metropolitan Melbourne in levels that require major attention. During my fifteen-year construction career in Melbourne, I haven't encountered any air moisture problem that couldn't be mitigated by the occupants' lifestyle or simply by the installation of an additional exhaust fan. The difference between the indoor and outdoor temperature and poor sealing, even in most new homes today, means that there is not enough moisture build-up to produce enough condensation to cause concern. We are lucky to be just above the point of concern most of the year.

I have, however, noted significant moisture problems in the outskirts of Melbourne, in Olinda and other parts of the Dandenongs, which have a few degrees lower average annual temperature than most of Melbourne. Also, the whole of Tasmania and the alpine region of Victoria and NSW are regions of concern.

A completely different problem is present in Australian tropical regions. There, the outdoor moisture is greater than what we have in artificially cooled indoor spaces, and so moisture migrates in the opposite direction.

Other often-encountered moisture problems are

damp and poorly ventilated subfloor spaces. This results in an unpleasant smell inside the house. The Australian Building Code regulates exactly the number of openings needed in the subfloor area to mitigate this problem. However, often after houses are built, additional outdoor landscaping works cause the outdoor ground level to be higher than under the house, and sometimes wrongly laid concrete paving streams rainwater directly under the house—an extremely difficult and expensive situation to rectify. One way is to create forced subfloor ventilation by installing fans that provide additional airflow in the subfloor area. Houses with moist subfloors are also more likely to be affected by termites.

One of the top insurance claims are leaking balconies and showers—more often than not caused by poor construction. Nothing works better against leaking balconies and showers than good design and an experienced builder. Water is a slow and very persistent element and should be treated with great caution. Properly executed waterproofing measures take a holistic approach to mitigating water flow. Sometimes I refuse work if it's poorly designed by a client's architects. When leaking occurs, nobody calls the architect …

Heating and cooling

It is possible (and relatively simple) to build a house in Australia without needing any form of artificial heating or cooling. However, there are a few peaks in the middle of winter and summer which make this option disproportionally expensive, so it's best to strike a good compromise between a well-performing house and a minimal need for heating or cooling.

Until recently natural gas has been the alpha and omega of heat in Australia, providing fuel for heating, cooking and hot water. Now, however, gas is starting to get expensive, and the government is slowly beginning to phase out connecting natural gas to new houses. Some large energy companies are pushing to replace natural gas with green hydrogen (a whole new [suburb in South Australia will be connected to hydrogen](). However, it will most likely be difficult to use the existing gas network in Australian cities for hydrogen. The main reason is that hydrogen is the smallest atom of all elements and tends to leak through most other materials, and the existing gas network and appliances just won't be able to cope with this.

The future of heating Australian homes is in heat-pump technology, which has made big progress in the last few decades. Refrigerators have heat pumps. They work by 'pumping' heat from inside the fridge to the back of the fridge where we can feel the heat. Reverse-cycle air conditioners work in the same way; the only difference is that we can reverse the cycle and pump the heat in or out of the house and consequently warm up or cool down the house as we please. The vast majority of heat pumps sold in Australia are in the form of reverse-cycle air conditioners with internal and external units connected with copper pipes. There is growing popularity and some government subsidies for heat-pump water heaters. Heat-pump water heaters were, until very recently, mainly installed in the countryside in properties without access to the gas network. However, they are becoming more popular in metropolitan Melbourne.

My favourite, and the most comfortable, silent and healthy form of heating one can imagine, is a heat pump producing hot water pumped in pipes under the floor.

A considerable number of Melbourne homes still heat with solid fuels, mainly firewood, but occasionally a not-very-pleasant smell around my home in the winter months indicates that at least some coal is in use in some homes. In Europe and North America, solid fuels are most often burned in a room dedicated for heating equipment and hot water is pumped in radiators or under floor. They use logs or small wood pellets with a fully automated feeding system requiring little supervision. Solid fuel burners in Melbourne mostly use logs in the main living area and must be constantly fed. There is some charm in watching a fire burning. However, even the best wood burners and flues don't completely eliminate the always-present smell.

Another downside in our suburbs is the dust particles generated by many wood burners. In areas without much wind, these can potentially cause breathing problems in some people. In some cases dust particles also act as a condensation nucleus in which air moisture condenses and creates fog.

Heating with wood is carbon neutral. We simply use the sun's energy stored by photosynthesis in the wood. The CO_2 emissions are the same as what was pulled from the atmosphere while the tree was growing, and unburned logs would emit CO_2 when rotting in nature as part of the natural cycle. Our current CO_2 problems are generated by burning fossil fuels, which represent CO_2 drawn from the atmosphere many millions of years ago and stored in carbon, oil and gas.

The Insulation Go-to for Energy Saving

We all know about energy star ratings. It's on our fridges and washing machines, and it also applies to our homes. More stars equal better value—or does it?

Currently in Australia, houses must be built to a 6-star rating, with the energy rating completed by qualified energy raters who asses the house size, orientation, the number of north-facing windows, and the quality of the windows. And they determine what R-value insulation we need.

What is an R-value?

Put simply, the R-value is the unit of measurement that tells you how efficient an insulation system is. The higher the R-value, the more effective the insulation.

The R-value is determined by measuring the heat flow and resistance to heat flow between two plates, one hot and one cold, with the testing material between these two plates. CSIRO has a specialized laboratory and equipment in which to conduct such measurements and provide a rating to tested material.

The problem is that our homes lose heat in three

ways: conduction, convection and radiation. An R-value rating determined by CSIRO only measures conduction, while ignoring convection and radiation.

The issue with all fibrous insulation materials commonly used in Australia today, such as rock wool, glass wool, and blow-in cellulose, is that their value (stated on the product packaging) ignores airflow travelling through this material (convection). Convection or airflow significantly contributes to heat losses and our energy bill in the winter months.

What's the solution?

This is where the insulation material spray foam (SPF) or polyurethane foam comes in. When sprayed, it expands and perfectly seals all surfaces and gaps. By filling every crack and crevice, spray foam stops air leakage and deters the growth of mould and mildew.

Spray foam is categorised into two main types: open-cell spray foam and closed-cell spray foam. The latter, which is composed of cells that are completely closed, has an extremely high density, making it better at keeping the heat in and out of structures. That's why it's more commonly used in exterior applications, while open-cell spray foam is best suited to interior applications like wall cavities, crawl spaces and attics.

We have noticed that homes with spray foam insulation perform much better than the average, according to the stated R-value as measured by today's standard testing methods.

Although spray foam is more expensive than fibrous insulation, it can lead to bigger savings on your heating and cooling costs down the line. For example, by preventing heat from leaving your home, your heating system won't have to work as hard to keep your space at a comfortable temperature.

The winter months are a chilly, albeit timely, reminder of how important insulation is. And to have a home that truly performs well, you need to think beyond today's commonly accepted methods—even by the otherwise remarkable research organisations such as CSIRO. If you invest in efficient insulation, you will save money on energy bills.

Toto Properties has partnered with one of only two spray-foam insulation providers in Melbourne. Contact us today to talk to our experts and learn about how we can include it in your dream home.

13
The Psychology Underlying our Decisions

By Dr Nada Trtnik

How many decisions do we make based on rationality, and how many based on emotions? Why do we sometimes make irrational decisions? And what role do emotions play in the decision-making process (when partners make decisions as well)?

People make many different decisions every day. When it comes to choosing and deciding, people are inclined to accept the best option, given the various circumstances.

When people make decisions, they go through a decision-making process. The process of choosing low-value goods is different from the process of choosing durable high-value goods, such as housing.

People need a place to live. A living space is one of the

main and essential necessities in life, like food and clothes.

Home construction or home renovation is one of the most important life decisions for individuals, couples and families. Usually in life these decisions are few and rare, and therefore people don't have much experience in this particular field. Which means we have to learn new things, like how to go through the selection process to get to the final product. Housing decisions have a long-term effect. They are financially intensive, as they are usually tied to long-term funding, and they play a strong emotional and personal role. It's common for people to strongly identify with their home; for many it represents an extension of their identity; it can represent their personality and/or status.

The purpose of prudent decision-making and builder selection is to *maximize the benefits* of choice for both the client and the contractor. People want to make *good decisions*, the right decisions with which they'll be happy. When we choose one option, we usually discard the other options, and therefore we want to make the right decision. People don't like to lose out by making bad decisions.

The initial phase of the decision-making process is the *recognised need*, in this context, the desire to build a home or renovate or build additions to the existing home.

What follows is *research* for the necessary information. We need to research how much we can afford to spend on the desired project, what timeframe will be needed, and what kind of experts and documents we'll need. We collect information about the builders and architects. We consult and *obtain* estimates and the necessary data. A lot of information may already be stored in our memory bank, as we might have faced choosing a builder in the past, or heard from loved ones who went through a similar process, or we might have read something about the right way to choose a builder.

Often in the initial phase we tend to look for information in our environment; we ask our relatives, acquaintances, friends, neighbours, and others who've had similar experiences recently. Positive information from people we trust has a lot of power and influence in the decision-making process. If we don't have enough information about the construction service providers stored in our memory or from our environment, then we tend to search for them on the internet, or we visit construction-material stores and ask them for more information and about relevant contractors.

During the collection-of-information process, the individual collects various offers. Based on the offers, written or oral, the individual then *assesses* the various options. Judging the options is a process in which we weigh and compare the different collected options, either on our own or with the help of a partner or friends. Based on the collected information, the individual then assesses which contractor will provide them with the greatest benefits, according to the individual's expectations, needs and the line of fewest complications.

Towards the end of the selection process, we eliminate the less-suitable providers and select the more-suitable builders. What follows is the decision on which builder to use for the project. We carry out the building project with the builder we selected as the one best suited to our project. When an individual or a couple chooses the best-suited builder for their home project, and the implementation process begins, we weigh our choice in terms of the implementation itself, the cooperation with the builder, and our satisfaction with the overall planning. We judge our choice based on whether we're satisfied or less satisfied, or unsatisfied and disappointed. This process is the ongoing *assessment* present during the construction process and after the project is completed.

The individual must carefully consider their options in choosing a builder as the construction work usually involves large sums of investment, decisions which will carry long-term consequences, and mistakes are harder to correct further down the line. It's important to take the time to make this decision, to think logically and to identify our emotional motives.

Our choices are influenced by our rational judgement and, more often than not, our emotional, unconscious motives.

The decision-making process when choosing a service or goods of greater value that have a lasting effect on our lives is therefore influenced by our rational decision-making process and other psychological factors. People often think they make rational decisions but don't consider and explore the emotions that play a strong role in the decision-making process. Research finds that emotions have a greater impact on our decision-making than reason and logic.

When designing a home, everyone has their own expectations, which are limited to financial availability, construction capabilities and visual manifestation.

When making decisions about building a home, renovating and choosing a builder, take the time to make an appropriate judgement of the situation. A pen and paper are a very useful way of determining that. Write down your wishes, expectations and possible problems. Write down what you want and what you don't want. The more time you take for the rational thinking process about the project, either by yourself or together with your household members, the better decisions you'll make, and the better prepared you'll be. The less ready you are, the less you'll think it through, and the more weight you'll leave to the emotional decision-making process. Which can be bad, even impulsive. People often indulge in emotional decision-making when they're insecure, indecisive, or confused, and they don't take enough time to think of their priorities. Emotional decision-making is considered faster and easier. But it's often worse.

You must be aware that the process of choosing an architect, a builder, and even the entire housing construction or renovation project is a stressful, demanding process. Prudence is necessary, and the more reflection you do, the better the outcome will be. Although deciding to build a home is a big life project, with a large financial investment for which the client often has to work for many years after building/buying a home, many people still make this big decision based on emotions and too little on rational thinking. Research estimates that 80% of decisions are still taken mainly based on emotions, which are influenced by psychological factors. These psychological factors play an important role because we didn't do enough rational assessment of the whole process of buying/building a house.

When assessing the possibilities, people take into account a number of rational aspects, which they assess and evaluate according to the criteria, such as:

- **Technical**: appearance of the contractor's products, contractor's reliability in relation to recommendations, forums, customers' feedback and quality.

- **Economic**: the price of the service, price of materials, final price, other possible additional costs, discounts and, of course, the client's available finances for the home project.

- **Social**: social standing and affiliation, fashion …

- **Personal**: the contractor's self-image, how confidently and convincingly they act. On the other hand is the client's self-image, their emotional belief that they'll be able to express their opinion to the contractor, and that their opinions will be taken into account. And thirdly, that the client and the contractor will be able to communicate in an inclusive way, morality (for example if the client finds out that the contractor has been part of risky or illegal transactions, or has cheated someone …), feelings of trust/distrust that the client experiences while making decisions, and contacting the potential builder, client's need for reassurance, risks.

Emotions play a very strong role in our decision-making processes. The human subconscious mind is influenced by many irrational beliefs, such as:

- People believe that the famous builders, for which we hear or read about (in magazines, ads, internet and from acquaintances) are better and of better quality. They can be. However, chances are they're just better at advertising themselves and their building company.

- The appearance of the construction products can look very appealing and beautiful on the outside. And if it's beautiful, people tend to think that the product is quality. People don't tend to think about the hidden flaws, sustainable quality and its functionality.

- The builder's verbal promise that there is no problem, that they will eliminate all hidden mistakes at their own expense, but if there is no written contract and something goes wrong, the builder can disappear and not fix the mistakes they promised to fix. People tend to have a lot of trust in the words of a confident and charismatic builder.

- Market beliefs that bigger builders have better prices than smaller ones.

- The ratio between price and quality, the idea that the more expensive products are also of better quality. This is not always the case.

- The positive recommendations of people we know, respect and appreciate have a strong influence on our choices and the decisions we make. They inspire us with their sense of confidence, especially if they have a lot of knowledge in the field about which we are making decisions.

- Our choices are also influenced by physical attractiveness, and the first impression we get from talking to the potential builder. Attraction stimuli are more convincing and have more positive impact on the choices we make than the average impression.

- Make a list of priorities; what is important to you and to your partner, your priorities and what is important to you when it comes to the builder. Also make a list of what you don't want. As a result, you'll know more about what you want and what you don't want. Consider the strengths of the potential builder, as well as his weaknesses. Often people want to see only the benefits; we don't want losses or complications. But, as in life, usually everything comes in a package. Therefore, when making a decision, it's important to assess the ability of the builder to admit to their mistakes and look for solutions on how to solve the problem together. Ask the builder about their failures and the things they've learnt along the way in the construction industry.

- Emotional delusions can occur when we indulge in emotions and make decisions based only on our feelings, especially those influenced by our first impression.

For example: You want the construction finished in one year; you don't want it to be delayed. Therefore, ask the builder about the work's timetable, how many other projects the construction company is doing, and what is the workforce of employees and other subcontractors.

What are the factors that influence the selection of a particular builder or architect?

Ask the builder about their references from people for whom he's built a house or renovated an apartment in the last three years. If possible, have a look at their previous constructions; ask previous clients to give feedback about the work, cooperation, satisfaction or dissatisfaction with the builder. Ask if the construction company has followed the timetables and deadlines, if the construction company communicated in advance about any delays, or if they just delayed without explanation. If they adhered to the contract in terms of implementation, price and deadlines. Ask the previous clients if something went wrong. Was the construction site clean and organised, or messy? Was the construction site very noisy, and how did the neighbours react? Does the construction company have an adequate network of subcontractors?

Practical advice on how to make the most optimal and rational decision

What reasons trigger the need to buy real estate or renovate a home?

- Leaving home, moving out of the parents' house, either alone or with a partner;
- Deciding to have a baby, or the birth of a baby/babies, and so requiring more space;
- Employment with an indefinite contract, consequently credit-worthiness, and a desire for one's own home;
- Separation and consequently the need for two separate units where the former partners can live separately, by themselves or with kids, after the divorce;
- Empty nest, when children grow up and move out, and the parents want to move to a smaller living unit;
- Aging people might prefer to live on the ground-floor apartment, for easier access, with no stairs;
- A desire for something new;
- The house getting so old that it makes no sense to renovate it;
- Better economic status and consequently the possibility of more luxurious housing, which might give the owner a greater sense of power and reputation.

Emotions that surface in the process of deciding to build a home or make a renovation

An individual, a couple or a family who decide to build a home face a variety of emotions. Firstly, there is excitement, the joy of anticipating a new home or remodelling an existing one. There are also fears and uncertainties about finances, how much to invest, which elements to add and which to give up. You will need courage, motivation and commitment in the search of the appropriate location. A suitable architect and builder with whom to make a conceptual design and concrete plans, and later the implementation. When choosing all the little and large built-in elements such as building materials, flooring, heating, design, roofing materials, doors, windows and so on, and when choosing furniture, each choice will require an assessment, weighing between major and minor benefits, which will be frustrating and exhausting. The client has to make a lot of choices and decisions, which can be stressful and can create a lot of uncertainty and need for additional research, consultation and decision making.

When choosing a builder, I believe it's really important to choose someone you can trust. Someone you can ask about their knowledge and opinions. When building a home, there will be a lot of decisions to make, and you need to be aware that each choice can have an impact on financial terms, upgrades, sustainability and overall satisfaction with the home.

Building and renovating a home requires a great deal of perseverance, on both parties, the client and the contractors.

Later, when children grow up, they will decide where to live their lives. They can live at home with their parents; they can rent a place; they can move into their partner's apartment or they can buy their own property. Some people buy real estate as an investment.

The decisions regarding the purchase of real estate are also influenced by external motivational factors. These factors could be the need for validation from others, showing off in front of others, a better reputation, higher status and so on.

About the Authors

Peter Mikus was born in 1973 in Slovenia and has been involved in the construction industry since childhood when he occasionally accompanied his father to his work in civil construction. He began his adult employment in hospitality, but when managing building works for his pizza shop, he discovered greater satisfaction in concrete than in tomato sauce.

He migrated to Australia in early 2000 and got his builder's licence in 2012 when he established Toto Properties, a construction company specialising in building on sloping land.

Peter is an advocate of sustainability, energy efficiency and healthy buildings that are kind to human health. He lives in Melbourne with his wife Gina and three children.

Dr Nada Trtnik, who wrote the final chapter, has a psychology practice in Slovenia that specialises in family relationships.

www.ingramcontent.com/pod-product-compliance
Lightning Source LLC
Chambersburg PA
CBHW041154110526
44590CB00027B/4229